Party

MOYRA FRASER

MEREHURST

LONDON

Contents

Managing Editor: Janet Illsley
Photographer: James Murphy
Designer: Sue Storey
Food Stylist: Maxine Clark
Photographic Stylist: Maria Jacques
Typeset by Maron Graphics Ltd, Wembley
Colour separation by Fotographics, UK - Hong Kong
Printed in Italy by New Interlitho S.p.A.

Published 1991 by Merehurst Ltd,
Ferry House, 51/57 Lacy Road, Putney, London SW15 1PR

© Merehurst Ltd

ISBN: 1 85391 181 X (Cased)
ISBN: 1 85391 250 6 (Paperback)

NOTES

All spoon measures are level: 1 tablespoon = 15ml spoon;
1 teaspoon = 5ml spoon.
Use fresh herbs and freshly ground black pepper unless otherwise stated.

Introduction

Everyone wants to give a successful party. The trick is to organise it in such a way that you can enjoy the occasion too. I think that the most difficult – but essential – aspect of giving a party is sitting down with pen in hand to plan the menu.

There are a number of things to consider first. How many people are you inviting? Do you want the party to be relaxed or formal? Do you have the space to seat everyone or will they be eating standing up? If they're standing, or balancing a plate on their knees, they must be able to pick up food easily using a fork or fingers.

Remember that any menu should be well balanced. Try to imagine the food being served together. Is it all one colour? Is it too creamy or too soft? The combination of dishes should present an interesting range of colour, flavour and texture. Try to make the most of fresh, plentiful seasonal foods, and any local specialities that can be included. Opt for food you feel relaxed cooking and serve it in a stylish way. Choose the main dish or dishes first, then select the accompaniments accordingly. The menu suggestions overleaf should help.

The question of how much to serve is often daunting and there are no hard and fast rules. The recipes have been devised so they can easily be doubled or multiplied further to cater for large numbers. In general, you will find that the more guests you have, the less food you need per head – especially if your guests are eating standing.

Finally, plan what you can do well ahead – one week in advance, the day before, etc. With a little forward planning, you'll be able to relax and enjoy your party as much as your guests will.

Mayr Fraser

Cold Buffet Menus

Celebration Buffet
Beef Niçoise
Smoked Salmon Roulade
Spiced Saffron Chicken
Cherry Tomato & Bean Salad
Mixed Grain & Mushroom Salad
leafy green salad
marinated mushrooms

Vegetarian Lunch
Chive Omelette Salad
Goat's Cheese & Sorrel Tart
grated carrot, cashew & orange
salad
assorted breads

Summer Garden Party
Lemon Ginger Chicken
Peppered Beef Fillet
Summer Vegetable Salad
Alfalfa & Apple Salad
Potato & Watercress Salad

Prepare-ahead Menu
Scallop & Avocado Salad
Creamed Spinach Terrine
mixed leaf salad
crusty brown bread

Wedding Buffet
Celebration Salmon
Spiced Saffron Chicken
Smoked Duck with Spiced Pears
Coconut Rice with Pineapple
Spiced Fennel & Avocado Salad
Spinach, Corn & Alfalfa Salad
Bean & Gruyère Salad

Quick & Easy Buffet
Devilled Duck Salad
Pear & Parmesan Salad
Cherry Tomato & Bean Salad
watercress & beansprout salad
warm rye bread

Hot Buffet Menus

Autumn Fork Buffet
Citrus Beef with Kumquats or
Beef & Mixed Mushroom Pot
steamed broccoli & broad beans
glazed carrots with ginger
creamed potatoes

Summer Barbecue
5-Spice Turkey Kebabs
Sausage & Potato Skewers
Marinated Prawns & Crab Claws
Cherry Tomato & Bean Salad
crisp green salad
hot herb bread

Hot Vegetarian Supper
Sweet Pepper & Basil Tranche
roasted new potatoes
oven-baked garlic mushrooms
julienne of carrot & parsnips
mixed leaf salad

Eastern Menu
Coconut Cream Chicken
Mixed Rice & Lentil Pilaff
cucumber & onion salad
sautéed spiced aubergines
(eggplant)

Winter Celebration
Beef en Croûte with Tapenade
Dauphinoise or jacket potatoes
sautéed mushrooms
glazed turnips

Prepare-ahead Feast
Smoked Chicken Lasagne
tomato salad with herbs
mixed leaf salad
French bread

NOTE: *Italicized accompaniments are suggestions, not recipes included within this book.*

Smoked Salmon Roulade

This is an elegant and economical way of serving smoked salmon and makes an attractive addition to the buffet table. I like to serve it with hot rye bread and a selection of salads.

If you use prawns and smoked salmon which haven't been previously frozen, this roulade can be frozen successfully. Defrost in the refrigerator overnight and slice while still partially frozen.

315g (10oz) thinly sliced smoked salmon
60g (2oz) peeled prawns, chopped
250g (8oz/1 cup) full-fat soft cheese
3 tablespoons chopped dill or chives

125g (4oz) unsalted butter, softened
2 tablespoons lemon juice
60ml (2 fl oz/¼ cup) single (light cream)
TO GARNISH:
rocket leaves
dill sprigs

1 Finely chop 60g (2oz) smoked salmon and place in a bowl with the remaining ingredients. Beat until evenly mixed, then cover and chill for about 1 hour.

2 Lay out the remaining smoked salmon on a large sheet of foil, overlapping the slices to form a rectangle 25 × 13cm (20 × 5 inches).

3 With wet hands, shape the cheese mixture into a roll about 25cm (10 inches) long and place in the centre of the smoked salmon. Roll the smoked salmon around the cheese filling to enclose it completely. Roll tightly in the foil and chill overnight.

4 Cut the roulade into thick slices and arrange on a serving platter. Garnish with rocket leaves and dill sprigs. Serve with lemon wedges. *Serves 8.*

Smokey Trout Mousse

A fish mousse is always a popular choice for a fork buffet. Smoked trout with apple may seem an unusual combination, but I'm sure you'll enjoy the partnership in this creamy mousse.

Include on your buffet menu one or two more substantial dishes, such as peppered beef fillet (page 25) and a choice of two or three salads.

250g (8oz) tart eating apples
185g (6oz) butter
500g (1lb) smoked trout fillets, skinned
625g (1¼lb) low-fat soft cheese
125ml (4 fl oz / ½ cup) lemon juice
315g (10oz / 1¼ cups) thick Greek yogurt

2 teaspoons powdered gelatine
pepper to taste
185g (6oz) bacon rashers, rinds removed
30g (1oz / ¼ cup) chopped hazelnuts, toasted
TO GARNISH:
tarragon sprigs

1 Peel, core and roughly chop the apples. Place in a saucepan with the butter and cook over a low heat until softened. Allow to cool.

2 Place the apple mixture, trout, soft cheese, lemon juice and yogurt in a food processor and work until smooth.

3 Put 2 tablespoons water in a small bowl. Sprinkle on the gelatine and leave until spongy, then stand the bowl in a small saucepan of hot water and leave for 4-5 minutes until the gelatine is completely dissolved. Add to the smoked trout mixture and process for a few seconds.

4 Spoon into a deep serving dish and leave in the refrigerator overnight to set.

5 Grill the bacon until very crisp, then crumble. Sprinkle the mousse with the bacon and nuts to serve. Garnish with tarragon and serve with toasted rye bread. *Serves 8.*

Scallop & Avocado Salad

This is an ideal dish for a light summer lunch party. Keep it simple and serve with a platter of smoked fish e.g. salmon, trout etc, a large mixed salad and plenty of interesting breads to accompany. Use fresh or frozen and thawed scallops.

1kg (2lb) scallops, halved
 horizontally
1 large red pepper, cored, seeded
 and cut into thin strips
1 large green pepper, cored,
 seeded and cut into thin strips
250g (8oz) red onion, thinly
 sliced
2 avocados
500g (1lb) tomatoes, peeled,
 seeded and cut into strips
TO GARNISH:
parsley or coriander sprigs
shredded lemon zest
thin lime slices

MARINADE:
1 clove garlic, crushed
2 tablespoons soft brown sugar
2 tablespoons chopped coriander
2 tablespoons chopped parsley
1/2 teaspoon salt
1/2 teaspoon coarse-ground black
 pepper
75ml (2½ fl oz / 1/3 cup) fresh
 lime juice
155ml (5 fl oz / 2/3 cup) lemon
 juice

1 For the marinade, whisk all of the ingredients together in a small bowl.

2 Place the scallops, peppers and onion in a large non-metallic dish. Pour over the marinade. Cover and leave to marinate in the refrigerator overnight.

3 Peel, halve and slice the avocados. Add to the scallop mixture with the tomatoes, and toss gently. Spoon on to a large serving platter and garnish with lemon zest, lime slices and herbs before serving. *Serves 6.*

Celebration Salmon

It's difficult to top salmon as a centrepiece for a special occasion buffet. This is definitely the best way of cooking a whole fish to serve cold. It never fails – the flesh is always beautifully moist and never overcooked.

If you haven't got a fish kettle or a roasting tin large enough to hold the salmon flat, curl it into a large preserving pan. It will keep its rounded shape after cooking and looks just as impressive when garnished.

1.75 kg (3½ lb) salmon or sea trout
60ml (2 fl oz / ¼ cup) white wine
½ onion, sliced
½ carrot, sliced
few black peppercorns

bay leaf
½ teaspoon powdered gelatine
4 tablespoons chopped dill
TO GARNISH:
lemon and lime slices
dill and parsley sprigs

1 Place the salmon or sea trout in a fish kettle or large roasting tin. Add the wine, onion, carrot, peppercorns and bay leaf. Pour over just enough cold water to cover the fish completely.

2 Bring just to the boil, then cover tightly with a lid or foil. Simmer very gently for 2 minutes, then turn off the heat and leave the fish in the liquid, still covered, to cool until lukewarm.

3 Carefully lift the warm salmon out of the poaching liquid on to a board. Strain the liquor, reserving 155ml (5 fl oz / ⅔ cup). Skin the fish and place on a large oval serving platter. Cover loosely with plastic wrap and place in the refrigerator.

4 Put the reserved liquor in a small bowl, sprinkle on the gelatine and leave to soften for 2-3 minutes. Stand the bowl in a saucepan of hot water and leave until dissolved.

5 Brush a little of this liquid over the cold salmon. Stir the chopped dill into the remaining liquid. Spoon evenly over the fish flesh to cover.

6 Serve the salmon or sea trout garnished with lemon and lime slices, dill and parsley sprigs. *Serves 8-10.*

Stir-fried Turkey Salad

I usually serve this salad on a bed of hot egg noodles or pasta tossed in olive oil, lemon juice and coarsely ground black pepper. It is excellent fork food for a party.

1 kg (2 lb) turkey fillets, cut into bite-sized pieces
MARINADE:
2 teaspoons caster sugar
1 teaspoon ground ginger
1 teaspoon turmeric
1 teaspoon curry powder
1 teaspoon chilli seasoning
1 teaspoon milk
'SALAD':
60 ml (2 fl oz / ¼ cup) grapeseed oil

500 g (1 lb) courgettes (zucchini), thinly sliced
375 g (12 oz) sugar snap peas
2 red peppers, cored, seeded and cut into strips
60 g (2 oz / ⅓ cup) cashew nuts
75 ml (2½ fl oz / ⅓ cup) lemon juice
60 ml (2 fl oz / ¼ cup) clear honey

1 First combine the ingredients for the marinade in a shallow dish. Add the turkey, toss well, cover and leave to marinate in a cool place overnight.

2 Heat half the oil in a large sauté pan or frying pan, add the courgettes (zucchini), sugar snap peas and red peppers and sauté for 3-4 minutes. Transfer to a large serving bowl.

3 Heat the remaining oil in the pan and sauté the turkey pieces, a few at a time, until golden. Return all the turkey to the pan and add the cashew nuts, lemon juice and honey.

4 Cook, stirring, for a further 3-4 minutes or until the turkey is tender. Toss into the vegetables and serve warm or cold, on a bed of hot egg noodles if you like. *Serves 8.*

Spiced Saffron Chicken

For chicken salads, I always prefer to poach the chicken – the flesh is much more moist and succulent than it is roasted. There's the bonus of stock for the freezer, too. Serve the salad on a bed of coconut rice with pineapple (page 74), accompanied by a selection of salads.

1 chicken, weighing 2kg (4lb)
light stock or water for poaching
bouquet garni
handful of flavouring
  ingredients (chopped onion,
  carrot, celery)
30g (1oz) butter
125g (4oz) onion, finely chopped
30g (1oz/¼ cup) no-soak dried
  apricots, chopped
grated rind of 1 lemon

½ teaspoon powdered saffron
155ml (5 fl oz/⅔ cup) dry white
  wine
2 tablespoons honey
1 teaspoon curry paste
155ml (5 fl oz/⅔ cup)
  mayonnaise
155ml (5 fl oz/⅔ cup) thick sour
  cream
salt and pepper to taste
coriander sprigs to garnish

1 Poach the chicken in stock or water to cover, with the bouquet garni and flavouring ingredients added, until tender. Leave to cool in the liquid.

2 Melt the butter in a pan, add the onion and cook gently until soft. Add the apricots, lemon rind, saffron, wine, honey and curry paste. Bring to the boil, then lower the heat and simmer for 8-10 minutes until the consistency of chutney. Cool.

3 Transfer the mixture to a food processor or blender and work until smooth. Turn into a large bowl and stir in the mayonnaise and sour cream. Season.

4 Lift the chicken out of the poaching liquid and remove all of the flesh, discarding the skin and bone. Cut into bite-sized pieces and fold into the spiced mayonnaise. Serve garnished with coriander, on a bed of rice salad. *Serves 8.*

Lemon Ginger Chicken

Definitely my favourite summer party dish – chicken fillets steeped in lemon juice and topped with a crispy sugar coating. Try using duck too. Serve it with mixed grain and mushroom salad (page 76) and a leafy salad.

750g(1½lb) chicken breast fillets
220ml (7 fl oz/⅞ cup) lemon
  juice
2 cloves garlic, crushed
2.5cm (1 inch) piece fresh root
  (green) ginger, sliced
1 stalk lemon grass (optional)
60ml (2 fl oz/¼ cup) grapeseed
  oil
90ml (3 fl oz/⅓ cup) chicken
  stock
60g (2 oz/⅓ cup) soft brown
  sugar

LEMON MAYONNAISE:
75ml (2½ fl oz/⅓ cup)
  mayonnaise
155ml (5 fl oz/⅔ cup) thick sour
  cream
60ml (2 fl oz/¼ cup) milk
salt and pepper to taste
grated rind of 1 lemon
TO GARNISH:
lemon wedges
coriander or parsley sprigs

1 Place the chicken, lemon juice, garlic, ginger and lemon grass if using, in a large non-metallic bowl. Mix well, cover and leave to marinate in the refrigerator overnight.
2 Drain the chicken, reserving the marinade. Heat half the oil in a large non-stick frying pan and brown the chicken a few pieces at a time, adding more oil as necessary.
3 Return all the chicken to the pan, and add the marinade and stock. Simmer, uncovered, for 10-12 minutes until the chicken is tender. Remove from the heat and leave to cool in the liquid.
4 Preheat the grill to high. Drain the chicken pieces and place in the grill pan. Sprinkle with the sugar and grill for a few minutes on each side until crisp and golden.
5 In a small bowl, mix together the mayonnaise, sour cream, milk, seasoning and lemon rind. Serve the warm chicken on a bed of rice salad, accompanied by the lemon mayonnaise.
Serves 8.

Smoked Duck & Spiced Pears

Smoked meats with hot pickled fruits is an excellent partnership. I often serve smoked gammon with pickled peaches, or smoked turkey with pickled prunes. Smoked duck is a delicious rich and tender meat; very popular in France, you'll find it ready sliced and pre-packed here in good delicatessens.

Served with hot ginger pears, smoked duck is absolutely delicious, perfect for serving alongside another cold meat platter such as sliced baked gammon.

220ml (7 fl oz / ¾ cup) distilled malt vinegar
2 whole allspice
6 black peppercorns
1 clove
1 stick cinnamon
2.5cm (1 inch) piece fresh root (green) ginger, sliced
pared rind of 1 lemon

1 tablespoon honey
125g (4oz / ½ cup) granulated sugar
6 ripe red-skinned dessert pears
2 bunches watercress
2 heads chicory (witlof)
750g (1½lb) smoked sliced duck breast

1 Place the vinegar, allspice, peppercorns, clove, cinnamon, ginger, lemon rind, honey and sugar in a large saucepan. Stir over a low heat until the sugar has completely dissolved. Bring to the boil and boil steadily for 2-3 minutes. Leave to cool, then strain into a large bowl.

2 Halve, core and slice the pears. Add to the spiced liquid, cover and leave overnight.

3 Roughly chop the watercress and chicory (witlof). Place in a bowl and add the pears, together with about 60ml (2 fl oz/ ¼ cup) of the spiced liquid; toss lightly.

4 Arrange the spiced pear salad on a large serving platter with the smoked duck slices. Serve the remaining liquid separately. *Serves 6.*

Devilled Duck Salad

This colourful salad is delicious accompanied by a fresh mango 'chutney' of chopped fresh mango, a little chopped onion and fresh coriander. Serve warm rye bread to mop up the tasty dressing, and side salads too.

The duck breasts can be cooked in advance and enjoyed cold but I prefer to cook them at the last minute and serve warm.

8 skinned duckling breasts, each
  about 155g (5oz)
2 tablespoons ground coriander
2 teaspoons ground ginger
2 teaspoons ground mace
1 clove garlic, crushed
125ml (4 fl oz / ½ cup) fresh
  orange juice
315ml (10 fl oz / 1¼ cups)
  olive oil

1 tablespoon honey
2 tablespoons red wine vinegar
1 tablespoon Dijon mustard
salt and pepper to taste
TO SERVE:
mixed salad leaves, such as frisée
  (curly endive), oakleaf lettuce,
  radicchio
black olives
coriander sprigs

1 Preheat the oven to 200C (400F / Gas 6). Place the duckling breasts in a shallow ovenproof dish. In a small bowl, mix the spices and garlic with 2 tablespoons each of orange juice and oil. Spread this mixture over the duckling breasts and roast for 20 minutes or until the duckling is tender and well browned.

2 To make the dressing, whisk together the remaining orange juice and oil with the honey, vinegar, mustard and seasoning.

3 Cover a platter with a bed of mixed salad leaves. Thickly slice the duck breasts and arrange on the salad. Scatter black olives on top and spoon over half of the dressing. Garnish with coriander and serve the remaining dressing separately. *Serves 8.*

Peppered Beef Fillet

I usually start this beef dish two days before required. I marinate it one day, cook it the next then keep it in the refrigerator until required. By this time the beef has absorbed all the flavours of the marinade. It is also firmer when chilled – making it easy to carve into wafer-thin slices. Serve with a selection of simple salad accompaniments.

1.25kg (2½lb) fillet of beef
1 teaspoon each dried pink and black peppercorns, coarsely ground
90ml (3 fl oz / ⅓ cup) grapeseed oil
1 clove garlic, crushed
2 teaspoons ground ginger
3 tablespoons wholegrain mustard
1 tablespoon light soft brown sugar

HERB DRESSING:
220ml (7 fl oz / ⅞ cup) olive oil
3 tablespoons lemon juice
2 tablespoons each chopped parsley, basil and marjoram
3 drops Tabasco sauce
salt and pepper to taste
TO SERVE:
mixed salad leaves, such as roquette, lamb's lettuce (corn salad) and cress

1 Roll up the beef and tie at 2.5cm (1 inch) intervals with fine string. Place in a non-metallic dish. In a small bowl, mix together the peppercorns, oil, garlic, ginger, mustard and sugar. Spread this mixture all over the beef fillet. Cover loosely and refrigerate overnight.

2 Preheat the oven to 220C (425F/Gas 7). Transfer the beef and marinade to a small roasting tin and roast, basting occasionally, for 40 minutes for medium-rare beef. (Cook for an extra 5-7 minutes for well done meat).

3 Remove from the oven and leave to cool, basting with the residual pan juices occasionally.

4 For the herb dressing, whisk together all the ingredients in a small bowl, with the remaining pan juices. Carve the beef into wafer-thin slices and arrange on a platter lined with mixed salad leaves. Serve the herb dressing separately.

Serves 8-10.

Beef Nicoise

An updated version of the well-loved classic salad niçoise. At first glance there appears to be too much dressing, but you'll find that when the salad is left to marinate overnight most of the dressing is absorbed – to delicious effect!

2 tablespoons grapeseed oil
750g (1½lb) fillet of beef
375g (12oz) French beans
500g (1lb) new potatoes
20 black olives, pitted
500g (1lb) cherry tomatoes,
  halved

TO GARNISH:
flat-leaved parsley
whole cherry tomatoes

DRESSING:
185ml (6 fl oz / ¾ cup) olive oil
3 tablespoons white wine vinegar
½ teaspoon caster sugar
2 teaspoons Dijon mustard
1 tablespoon wholegrain
  mustard
2 tablespoons chopped parsley
salt and pepper to taste

1 First whisk together all the ingredients for the dressing in a small bowl and set aside.

2 Preheat the oven to 200C (400F/Gas 6). Heat the grapeseed oil in a frying pan, add the fillet and quickly brown on all sides. Transfer to a roasting tin and cook in the oven for 15-20 minutes, until medium-rare. Cool, then cut into thin finger-length strips.

3 Cook the French beans in boiling salted water for 5-7 minutes or until just tender; drain. Cook the potatoes in boiling salted water for 10-12 minutes until tender; drain.

4 Toss together the warm French beans and potatoes, beef, olives, tomatoes and dressing. Cover and refrigerate overnight. Bring to room temperature and stir well before serving. Garnish with flat-leaved parsley and whole cherry tomatoes. *Serves 6.*

Chive Omelette Salad

This is an excellent vegetarian option to include on any cold buffet menu. Believe it or not, cold shredded omelette is delicious tossed into a salad. The omelettes, dressing and salad ingredients for this dish can be prepared ahead and mixed together when ready to serve.

4 eggs
2 tablespoons chopped chives
salt and pepper to taste
2 tablespoons olive oil
DRESSING:
140ml (4½ fl oz / ½ cup) olive oil
1 teaspoon Dijon mustard
2 tablespoons white wine vinegar
1 clove garlic, crushed
SALAD:
1 cucumber, cut into thin strips
250g (8oz) courgettes (zucchini),
  cut into thin strips

1 small iceberg lettuce, shredded
1 yellow pepper, cored, seeded
  and cut into strips
1 red pepper, cored, seeded and
  cut into strips
3 large tomatoes, quartered,
  seeded and cut into strips
125g (4oz / ¾ cup) black olives,
  pitted (optional)
TO GARNISH:
whole chives

1 For the omelettes, whisk together the eggs, chives and seasoning in a bowl. Heat 1-2 teaspoons of the oil in an omelette pan and add just enough egg mixture to cover the base of the pan. Cook for 1 minute, turn over and cook for a further 1 minute. Turn out on to a plate and leave to cool. Continue making omelettes in this way until all the egg mixture has been used. Roll up the cold omelettes and cover loosely until required.

2 For the dressing, whisk together all the ingredients in a bowl with seasoning.

3 When ready to serve, thinly slice the omelette rolls. Toss together all the salad ingredients on a serving platter. Add the shredded omelette and dressing. Toss gently and serve immediately, garnished with chives. *Serves 8.*

Goat's Cheese & Sorrel Tart

Even if you don't particularly like goat's cheese you can't fail to enjoy this creamy tart. Sorrel is a particular favourite of mine – I love its slightly sour flavour in cheesy dishes such as this. When it is out of season use fresh spinach, or frozen chopped spinach (well-drained) instead.

For a totally vegetarian option, serve with summer vegetable salad (page 64) and spinach, corn and alfalfa salad (page 70).

410g (13oz) packet shortcrust
* pastry*
30g (1oz) butter
60g (2oz) onion, finely chopped
1 clove garlic, crushed
60g (2oz) sorrel, chopped
185g (6oz) soft goat's cheese

2 eggs
155ml (5 fl oz / ⅔ cup) single
* (light) cream*
pinch of ground nutmeg
salt and pepper to taste
TO SERVE:
freshly grated gruyère cheese

1   Preheat the oven to 200C (400F / Gas 6). Roll out the pastry thinly on a lightly floured surface and use to line a 30 × 11cm (12 × 4½ inch) tranche tin. Chill for 15 minutes. Line with greaseproof paper and baking beans and bake blind for 15 minutes or until the pastry edges are pale golden. Remove the paper and beans and bake for a further 5 minutes to cook the base. Lower the oven temperature to 180C (350F / Gas 4).
2   Melt the butter in a sauté pan, add the onion and garlic and cook gently for 3-4 minutes until golden. Add the sorrel and cook for 1 minute until wilted.
3   In a large bowl, mix together the goat's cheese, eggs and cream until smooth. Stir in the sorrel mixture, nutmeg and seasoning. Spoon into the prepared flan case and bake for about 30 minutes or until golden and lightly set. Serve warm, topped with gruyère and accompanied by a crisp salad.
Serves 6.

NOTE: If you prefer to make your own pastry, use a 185g (6oz/ 1¼ cup) flour quantity. A 20cm (8 inch) flan tin can be used instead of a tranche tin.

Creamed Spinach Terrine

2 tablespoons freshly grated
  Parmesan cheese
1 tablespoon olive oil
4 spring onions (green shallots),
  finely chopped
1 clove garlic, crushed
250g (8oz) spinach, roughly
  chopped
375g (12oz) ricotta or other
  low-fat soft cheese
315ml (10 fl oz / 1¼ cups) double
  (thick) cream

3 eggs
salt and pepper to taste
DRESSING:
375g (12oz) ripe pears
155ml (5 fl oz / ⅔ cup) hazelnut
  oil
155ml (5 fl oz / ⅔ cup) olive oil
1 teaspoon red wine vinegar
TO GARNISH:
2 tablespoons chopped toasted
  hazelnuts
small spinach leaves

1 Preheat the oven to 180C (350F/Gas 4). Oil a 1.2 litre (2 pint) rectangular ovenproof terrine or loaf tin. Line the base and sides with non-stick paper. Lightly oil the paper and sprinkle with the Parmesan.

2 Heat the oil in a large sauté pan, add the spring onions (shallots) and garlic and sauté for 2-3 minutes. Add the spinach and continue to cook, stirring, until the spinach has wilted and all the excess liquid has evaporated.

3 Place the spinach mixture, ricotta cheese, cream, eggs and seasoning in a food processor or blender and work until smooth. Pour into the terrine and cover with buttered foil.

4 Place in a bain-marie, or a roasting tin containing enough water to come halfway up the sides of the tin. Bake in the oven for about 1½-2 hours or until a skewer inserted into the centre comes out clean. Cool in the terrine. Pour off any excess liquid, then chill for 2 hours.

5 To make the dressing, peel, halve and core the pears. Purée in a food processor or blender with the oils, vinegar and seasoning.

6 Serve the terrine thickly sliced with the dressing, and hazelnuts and spinach leaves to garnish. *Serves 8.*

Marinated Prawns & Crab Claws

These are delicious served with an aromatic saffron flavoured mayonnaise (see below).

1kg (2lb) medium-sized raw
prawns, tails shelled
12 cooked crab claws
90g (3 oz/³⁄4 cup) dry
breadcrumbs
MARINADE:
60ml (2 fl oz/¹⁄4 cup) olive oil
60ml (2 fl oz/¹⁄4 cup) grapeseed
oil
grated rind of 1 lemon

1 clove garlic, crushed
2.5cm (1 inch) piece fresh root
(green) ginger, chopped
2 tablespoons white wine vinegar
large pinch of chilli powder
1 teaspoon paprika
salt and pepper to taste
TO GARNISH:
lemon slices

1 First whisk together the marinade ingredients in a bowl.
2 Peel the prawns, leaving the tails on, and place in a large non-metallic dish. Pour over all but 4 tablespoons of the marinade. Cover the dish.
3 Crack the crab claw shells by tapping them lightly with a rolling pin. Peel away the shell to expose the flesh but leave 2.5cm (1 inch) of shell at the tip. Place in a separate dish and spoon the reserved marinade over the crab flesh. Cover and leave both the prawns and crab claws in the refrigerator overnight.
4 Drain the prawns, reserving the marinade. Thread on to small wooden skewers and toss in the breadcrumbs. Cook on the barbecue or under a preheated grill for about 2 minutes on each side, basting occasionally with the marinade.
5 Arrange the crab claws and prawns on a platter and garnish with lemon slices. Serve with the mayonnaise. *Serves 6.*

SAFFRON MAYONNAISE: Combine 315ml (10 fl oz/1¹⁄4 cups) mayonnaise with 250g (8oz) Greek strained yogurt. Sauté 60g (2oz) chopped onion, 1 crushed garlic clove and ½ teaspoon saffron powder in a little butter until soft. Add to the mayonnaise and purée in a blender or food processor.

Seafood Gratin

A delicious mixture of moist, succulent flakes of salmon with plump scallops, prawns and fennel. This combination with a creamed potato topping makes a perfect buffet lunch dish. Serve with bean and gruyère salad (page 68) and a tomato salad.

For a party I prepare it to the end of stage 4 the day before and leave in the refrigerator overnight.

500g (1 lb) salmon tail
155ml (5 fl oz / ⅔ cup) dry white
  wine
250g (8oz) small queen scallops
375g (12oz) Florence fennel,
  thinly sliced
125g (4oz) peeled prawns
125g (4oz) butter
60g (2oz / ½ cup) plain flour

75ml (2½ fl oz / ⅓ cup) single
  (light) cream
1 tablespoon chopped dill
salt and pepper to taste
1 kg (2 lb) old potatoes
125ml (4 fl oz / ½ cup) milk
beaten egg to glaze
dill sprigs to garnish

1 Place the salmon in a saucepan, pour over the wine and 375ml (12 fl oz/1½ cups) water. Bring almost to the boil, cover and simmer very gently until almost tender, about 10-12 minutes. Add the scallops and simmer for 1 minute. Strain the cooking liquor and reserve.

2 Cook the fennel in boiling salted water for 12 minutes; drain.

3 Skin and bone the salmon, then flake into a 1.75 litre (3 pint) large ovenproof dish. Scatter the scallops, prawns and fennel on top.

4 Melt half the butter in a saucepan. Add the flour and cook, stirring, for 1 minute. Stir in the reserved liquor. Bring to the boil, stirring, and simmer for 1 minute. Off the heat, beat in the cream, dill and seasoning. Pour over the fish.

5 Preheat the oven to 190C (375F/Gas 5). Cook the potatoes in boiling salted water until tender; drain and mash. Beat in the milk, remaining butter and seasoning. Spoon or pipe the potatoes over the fish. Brush lightly with egg.

6 Bake for 35-40 minutes or until golden brown and hot through. Garnish with dill sprigs. *Serves 8.*

Hot Salmon with Tarragon

The attraction of this dish lies in its speed and simplicity. If the medallions are prepared ahead and refrigerated, it takes less than 15 minutes to complete. I prefer to bone the salmon steaks and curl them to form neat medallions, but you can cook them as steaks if you prefer.

Serve with a selection of quick-to-cook vegetables such as fine asparagus, mange tout (snow peas) and new potatoes.

8 salmon steaks, each about
155g (5oz)
155g (5oz) butter
8 lime slices
1 small bunch tarragon

185ml (6 fl oz / ¾ cup) fish stock
(preferably salmon stock)
185ml (6 fl oz / ¾ cup) crème
fraîche
salt and pepper to taste

1 Preheat the oven to 220C (425F/Gas 7). Carefully remove the centre bone from each salmon steak and halve each steak to form 2 cutlets. Skin and curl these pairs of cutlets around each other to form small medallions. Secure with fine string.
2 Melt half the butter in a frying pan, add the salmon with the lime slices, and brown quickly on both sides.
3 Place each salmon medallion on a 20cm (8 inch) square of greaseproof paper. Add a lime slice, a sprig of tarragon and a little melted butter. Bring up the edges of the paper and twist to enclose the salmon. Tie with string. Cook in the oven for 10-15 minutes until just tender.
4 Meanwhile, add the remaining butter to the pan with the fish stock and crème fraîche. Bring to the boil and simmer for 3-4 minutes. Remove from the heat and add a little chopped tarragon to taste. Adjust the seasoning.
5 To serve, open out the salmon parcels and pour in a little of the cream sauce; serve the remainder separately. Garnish each parcel with a fresh sprig of tarragon. *Serves 8.*

Chicken & Mozzarella Gratin

This is an excellent dish to serve at a party and is easily doubled up. I'd serve a basket of hot garlic and herb bread, and a large mixed salad with it. Slice the chicken before cooking if your guests will be eating standing up.

1kg (2 lb) aubergines (eggplants)
about 4 tablespoons oil
750g (1½ lb) boneless chicken
* breasts, skinned*
1 egg, beaten
90g (3oz / ¾ cup) freshly grated
* Parmesan cheese*
1 clove garlic, crushed

250g (8oz) onion, finely chopped
400g (14oz) can chopped
* tomatoes*
2 teaspoons dried mixed herbs
pinch of sugar
salt and pepper to taste
220g (7oz) mozzarella cheese,
* sliced*

1 Preheat the oven to 190C (375F / Gas 5). Thickly slice the aubergines (eggplants). Cook in boiling salted water for 2-3 minutes or until just beginning to soften. Drain and refresh under cold water. Dry on absorbent kitchen paper.

2 Preheat the grill to high. Brush the aubergine (eggplant) slices lightly with oil and grill on both sides until lightly browned.

3 Dip the chicken into the beaten egg, then into the Parmesan cheese to coat. Heat 2 tablespoons oil in a large sauté pan, add the chicken and sauté until evenly browned; remove and set aside.

4 Heat a further 1 tablespoon oil in the sauté pan. Add the garlic and onion and cook, stirring, for 1-2 minutes, then stir in the tomatoes, mixed herbs, sugar and seasoning.

5 Spoon the sauce into a large, shallow ovenproof dish. Arrange overlapping rows of chicken, aubergine (eggplant) and mozzarella on top of the tomato sauce. Sprinkle with any remaining Parmesan cheese.

6 Bake, uncovered for 35-40 minutes or until golden brown and cooked through. *Serves 6.*

Coconut Cream Chicken

Don't be put off by the inclusion of green chilli in this dish; the sauce is very mild and creamy. Slice the chicken before serving if you want to serve it as fork food. Mixed rice and lentil pilaff (page 78) is an ideal accompaniment.

4 tablespoons oil
1.5kg (3 lb) boneless chicken
125g (4oz) onion, finely chopped
1 clove garlic, crushed
1 teaspoon each ground
  coriander, turmeric,
  paprika, mild curry powder
  and poppy seeds
60g (2oz) creamed coconut,
  grated

1-2 green chillis, finely sliced
185g (6oz) tomatoes, skinned,
  seeded and chopped
90ml (3 fl oz / ⅓ cup) double
  (thick) cream
salt and pepper to taste
TO GARNISH:
lime slices
coriander sprigs

1 Heat the oil in a large sauté pan, add the chicken and brown evenly; remove and set aside. Add the onion and garlic to the pan and cook, stirring, for 1-2 minutes. Stir in the spices, creamed coconut and chilli(s). Cook, stirring, for 1 minute.

2 Stir in the tomatoes, chicken and 250ml (8 fl oz/1 cup) water. Bring to the boil, cover and simmer for about 25 minutes.

3 Stir in the cream and simmer for 1-2 minutes; adjust the seasoning. Garnish with lime slices and coriander sprigs to serve. *Serves 8.*

Smoked Chicken Lasagne

This delicious rich creamy dish can be assembled the day before, ready to cook when required. Serve with a crisp green salad and warm French bread.

Don't be put off by the vast amount of sauce in this recipe – the pasta absorbs it during cooking!

185g (6oz) butter
500g (1 lb) brown cap
  mushrooms, sliced
2 tablespoons lemon juice
salt and pepper to taste
125g (4oz/1 cup) plain flour
1 litre (1¾ pints/4 cups) milk
1 litre (1¾ pints/4 cups) chicken
  stock
142g (5oz) packet full-fat soft
  cheese with herbs
90g (3oz) gruyère cheese, grated

1 clove garlic, crushed
250g (8oz) frozen chopped
  spinach, thawed
1kg (2lb) boneless poached
  chicken, skinned
250g (8oz) boneless smoked
  chicken, skinned
315g (10oz) quick-cook egg
  lasagne
60g (2oz/1 cup) fresh white
  breadcrumbs
chives to garnish

1 Preheat the oven to 200C (400F/Gas 6). Melt 60g (2oz) butter in a large saucepan. Add the mushrooms, lemon juice and seasoning. Cook, stirring, for 3-4 minutes, then remove the mushrooms with a slotted spoon and set aside.

2 Simmer the pan juices until reduced by about half, then add the remaining butter and heat until melted. Add the flour and cook, stirring, for 1 minute. Stir in the milk and stock, bring to the boil and simmer, stirring, for 1-2 minutes. Remove from the heat and beat in the soft cheese, gruyère, garlic, spinach and seasoning.

3 Cut both types of chicken into bite-sized pieces and mix together. Spoon a little of the sauce into one large, or two medium ovenproof dishes. Cover with a layer of lasagne, followed by chicken, mushrooms and sauce. Continue layering in this way, finishing with a layer of sauce. Sprinkle the breadcrumbs over the top.

4 Bake for 1-1¼ hours until golden and hot through. Garnish with chives to serve. *Serves 8-10.*

Five-Spice Turkey Kebabs

I've also used pork tenderloin in this recipe with equal success. Five-spice powder is often used in Chinese cooking and lends a delightful fragrant, aniseed flavour. If you can't find it however, use a mild curry powder.

Serve these tasty kebabs with a selection of salads and warm crusty bread.

750g (1½ lb) boneless turkey breasts, skinned
375g (12oz) aubergine (eggplant)
375g (12oz) streaky bacon rashers, rinds removed
2 small red onions, quartered and separated into layers
TO GARNISH:
cucumber slices

MARINADE:
1 teaspoon five-spice powder
125ml (4 fl oz / ½ cup) thin tahini paste
60ml (2 fl oz / ¼ cup) tomato ketchup
60ml (2 fl oz / ¼ cup) single (light) cream
1 tablespoon oil
2 large cloves garlic, crushed
1 tablespoon lemon juice

1 First whisk together all the marinade ingredients in a bowl.

2 Cut the turkey into 2.5cm (1 inch) cubes. Cut the aubergine (eggplant) into similar-sized pieces and blanch in boiling salted water for 1-2 minutes.

3 Stretch the bacon rashers with the back of a knife and cut each one in half. Wrap each turkey cube in bacon and thread on to wooden skewers, alternately with aubergine (eggplant) and onion pieces.

4 Place the kebabs in a single layer in a non-metallic dish. Spoon over the marinade, cover and leave to marinate in the refrigerator overnight.

5 Remove the kebabs from the marinade. Preheat the grill or barbecue and cook the kebabs for 10-12 minutes, basting and turning occasionally, until golden brown and cooked through. Serve garnished with cucumber slices. *Serves 8.*

Duckling & Cashew Nut Pilaff

Most supermarkets now sell duckling breasts but if you prefer, use chicken breast fillets instead. Slice the duckling before serving if you want to serve the pilaff as fork food.

75ml (2½ fl oz / ⅓ cup) olive oil
1kg (2lb) boneless duckling
  breasts, halved
90g (3oz / ⅔ cup) cashew nuts
375g (12oz) onion, chopped
1 green chilli, seeded and finely
  chopped
4 teaspoons ground coriander
2 cloves garlic, crushed
690ml (22 fl oz / 2¾ cups)
  chicken stock

625ml (1 pint / 2½ cups) dry
  cider
salt and pepper to taste
500g (1lb / 3 cups) long-grain
  white rice
3 tablespoons chopped parsley
TO GARNISH:
lemon slices
parsley sprigs

1 Preheat the oven to 160C (325F/Gas 3). Heat the oil in a large flameproof casserole. Add the duck pieces a few at a time with the cashew nuts and fry gently until a deep golden brown. Remove with a slotted spoon and set aside.

2 Add the onion to the casserole and cook, stirring, for 1-2 minutes. Add the chilli, coriander and garlic. Cook, stirring, for 1 minute. Add the stock, cider and seasoning. Bring to the boil.

3 Return all the duck pieces and cashew nuts to the pan. Cover tightly and cook in the oven for 45 minutes. Stir in the rice, cover and return to the oven for a further 35 minutes or until the rice is tender and most of the liquid absorbed. Stir in the parsley and adjust the seasoning. Serve garnished with lemon slices and parsley. *Serves 6.*

Honeyed Lamb Tagine

I find this lamb dish freezes very well. Leave it to thaw overnight at cool room temperature, then simply bring to a simmer for about 20 minutes before serving. A large bowl of steaming hot couscous, subtly flavoured with toasted almonds and pared lemon rind, is the perfect accompaniment.

2 thin-skinned lemons
5 tablespoons grapeseed oil
185g (6oz) onion, chopped
2 teaspoons honey
2 cloves garlic, crushed
2 teaspoons ground allspice
1 teaspoon ground cinnamon
pinch of chilli powder
*1 litre (1¾ pints / 4 cups) lamb
    stock*

*2 tablespoons tomato purée
    (paste)*
salt and pepper to taste
*1.5kg (3lb) boned leg of lamb,
    cubed*
60g (2oz / ½ cup) plain flour
4 firm pears
16 fresh dates, pitted
pared lemon zest to garnish

1 Preheat the oven to 160C (325F/Gas 3). Put the lemons in a saucepan, cover with cold water and bring to the boil. Cover and simmer for 10-12 minutes until softened; drain. Cut each lemon into 6 wedges.

2 Heat the oil in a frying pan, add the onion and honey and cook, stirring, over a low heat until soft and golden. Stir in the garlic, allspice, cinnamon and chilli powder. Cook, stirring, for 1 minute. Spoon into a deep casserole and add the stock, tomato purée (paste) and seasoning.

3 Toss the lamb in the seasoned flour and shake off any excess. Stir the lamb into the onion mixture with the lemon wedges. Cover and cook in the oven for 45 minutes.

4 Peel, quarter and core the pears and stir into the casserole with the dates. Add a little extra stock at this stage if the juices look too thick. Cover and return to the oven for a further 30-40 minutes or until the lamb is very tender.

5 Serve with plenty of steamed couscous and garnish with lemon zest. *Serves 8.*

Citrus Beef with Kumquats

A rich casserole with a hint of orange – ideal for hot winter buffets. Serve with a large dish of creamed potatoes or small jacket potatoes. A simple salad is the only extra accompaniment required; serve a selection of mixed salad leaves or spinach, corn and alfalfa salad.

1 kg (2 lb) stewing steak
salt and pepper to taste
60g (2oz / ½ cup) plain flour
3 tablespoons grapeseed oil
pared rind and juice of 1 orange
1 clove garlic, crushed
315ml (10 fl oz / 1¼ cups) beef
  stock

155ml (5 fl oz / ⅔ cup) red wine
1 bay leaf
375g (12oz) celery, thickly sliced
375g (12oz) leeks, thickly sliced
125g (4oz) kumquats
salad leaves to garnish

1 Preheat the oven to 160C (325F/Gas 3). Cut the beef into 2.5cm (1 inch) cubes and toss in the seasoned flour to coat evenly; shake off any excess flour. Heat the oil in a large flameproof casserole and quickly brown the beef, a few pieces at a time, on all sides.

2 Return all the beef to the pan. Add the pared orange rind, 3 tablespoons orange juice, garlic, stock, wine, bay leaf and seasoning. Bring to a simmer, cover and cook in the oven for 1 hour.

3 Add the celery, leeks and kumquats, cover and return to the oven for a further 1½ hours or until the beef is very tender. Adjust the seasoning. Serve garnished with salad leaves. *Serves 6.*

Beef & Mixed Mushroom Pot

I usually try to buy the smoked streaky bacon in one piece from my local butcher, and cut it into thick strips. This is a good dish to have made and ready in the freezer for hot fork meals. Rice flavoured with toasted nuts and herbs is an ideal accompaniment.

1 kg (2 lb) stewing beef, cubed
salt and pepper to taste
60g (2oz / ½ cup) plain flour
4 tablespoons grapeseed oil
250g (8oz) button onions, peeled
185g (6oz) smoked streaky
   bacon, rinds removed, thinly
   sliced
625ml (1 pint / 2½ cups) beef
   stock
500g (1 lb) mixed mushrooms eg.
   brown cap, chanterelles, ceps,
   parasols, oyster mushrooms

MARINADE:
1 small onion, sliced
1 small carrot, sliced
1 stick celery, sliced
1 clove garlic, crushed
470ml (15 fl oz / 2 cups) red wine
6 juniper berries, crushed
2 tablespoons olive oil
few thyme sprigs
TO GARNISH:
thyme sprigs
parsley sprigs

1 First place all the marinade ingredients in a non-metallic bowl. Cut the beef into 4cm (1½ inch) cubes and add to the marinade. Stir well, cover and leave to marinate in the refrigerator overnight.

2 Preheat the oven to 160C (325F / Gas 3). Remove the beef from the marinade with a slotted spoon; drain. Toss the beef in the seasoned flour to coat evenly, shaking off excess flour. Strain the marinade and reserve. Heat the oil in a large flameproof casserole and quickly brown the beef, a few pieces at a time, on all sides.

3 Return all the beef to the pan. Add the strained marinade and all the remaining ingredients, except the mushrooms. Bring to the boil, cover and cook in the oven for 2 hours.

4 Add the mushrooms, cover and return to the oven for a further 30 minutes or until the beef is very tender. Adjust seasoning. Serve garnished with thyme and parsley. *Serves 6.*

Beef en Croûte with Tapenade

This is a much lighter version of the traditional beef en croûte. I flavour mine with tapenade which is a delicious olive paste quite widely available now, both in delicatessens and major super-markets. You can of course omit the tapenade if you prefer.

Serve with glazed turnips and sautéed mushrooms, or green vege-tables, such as broccoli and broad beans, and a gratin of potatoes.

2 tablespoons oil	salt
1 kg (2lb) piece middle cut fillet of beef	1 tablespoon coarse-ground black pepper
60g (2oz / ⅓ cup) tapenade	142 ml (5 fl oz / ⅔ cup) thick sour cream
4 large sheets filo pastry	
90g (3oz) butter, melted	rosemary sprigs to garnish

1 Preheat the oven to 220C (425F/Gas 7). Heat the oil in a frying pan, then add the meat and brown quickly on all sides. Remove and leave to cool and drain on absorbent kitchen paper.

2 Set aside 1 tablespoon tapenade for the tapenade cream. Place a sheet of filo pastry on the work surface and brush lightly with melted butter. Spread with 1 tablespoon tapen-ade and place another sheet of filo on top. Continue layering the filo, melted butter and tapenade in this way, finishing with tapenade.

3 Place the fillet of beef on top, season and fold the filo pastry over the beef to enclose. Trim off any excess pastry. Place the croûte, seam side down, on a baking sheet. Decorate with leaves cut from the pastry trimmings. Brush with the re-maining melted butter. Sprinkle with the black pepper.

4 Bake for 30 minutes, covering lightly with foil if the pastry appears to be browning too quickly. The meat will be med-ium rare after this time; cook for a little longer if you prefer.

5 Meanwhile, in a bowl beat together the reserved tapenade and sour cream. Cover and refrigerate until required.

6 Serve the croûte garnished with rosemary sprigs. Hand the tapenade cream around separately. *Serves 6.*

Nasi Goreng

This is an Indonesian dish found on most Malaysian menus but with varying ingredients and flavours. I would complete the dish ahead of time then reheat in a hot oven in a well-buttered dish covered with buttered foil for about 35 minutes.

500g (1lb/3 cups) long-grain
  white rice
salt and pepper to taste
4 eggs, beaten
75ml (2½ fl oz / ⅓ cup) grapeseed
  oil
2 bunches spring onions (green
  shallots), cut into 4cm
  (1½ inch) lengths
6 red peppers, cored, seeded and
  roughly chopped
2 green peppers, cored, seeded
  and roughly chopped

1 teaspoon ground turmeric
½ teaspoon chilli powder
125g (4oz) frozen peas
500g (1lb) cooked beef or pork,
  cut into very thin strips
125g (4oz) peeled prawns
1cm (½ inch) piece fresh root
  (green) ginger, finely chopped
1 clove garlic, crushed
2 tablespoons soy sauce

1 Cook the rice in boiling salted water until just tender; drain if necessary.

2 For the omelettes, whisk together the eggs, 2 tablespoons water and seasoning. Heat 1-2 teaspoons of the oil in an omelette pan and add a third of the egg mixture. Cook for 1 minute, turn over and cook the other side for 1 minute. Turn on to a plate. Repeat to make two more omelettes, then roll up the omelettes and set aside.

3 Heat remaining oil in a large frying pan or wok. Add the spring onions (shallots), peppers and spices. Stir over a high heat for 1-2 minutes. Add the rice, peas, beef or pork, prawns, ginger and garlic. Continue to cook, stirring over a high heat, for a further 2-3 minutes.

4 Thinly slice the omelette rolls. Add the soy sauce and omelette shreds to the mixture and stir-fry for a further 2 minutes. *Serves 8-10.*

Sausage & Potato Skewers

For these I usually buy homemade spicy pork sausages from my local Italian delicatessen, or choose a good quality pork sausage from the butcher or supermarket.

Serve with hot pitta bread and simple side salads, such as cherry tomato and bean salad (page 68) and apple, leaf and walnut salad (page 64).

12 button onions, peeled
12 small new potatoes
750g (1½lb) coarse pork
* sausages*
TO SERVE:
small mint leaves
shredded spring onion (green
* shallot)*
pitta bread

MARINADE:
315ml (10 fl oz / 1¼ cups) Greek
* strained yogurt*
pinch of turmeric
1 tablespoon chopped mint
3 tablespoons olive oil
2 tablespoons honey
salt and pepper to taste

1 Simmer the button onions and new potatoes in salted water until almost tender, about 5 minutes. Drain well. Cut each sausage into 4cm (1½ inch) lengths.

2 Beat together the marinade ingredients. Add the sausage pieces, onions and potatoes. Stir well, cover and refrigerate overnight.

3 Preheat the grill or barbecue to high. Remove the sausage, onions and potatoes from the marinade with a slotted spoon. Strain the marinade and reserve. Thread the sausage, onions and potatoes alternately on to small wooden skewers. Grill or barbecue for 7-10 minutes, turning occasionally and basting frequently with the marinade.

4 Serve the skewers sprinkled with mint and accompanied by shredded spring onion (shallot) and hot pitta bread. *Serves 6.*

Sweet Pepper & Basil Tranche

Loose-based oblong fluted tranche tins are excellent for all kinds of flans – sweet and savoury. They cook evenly and the flans are easy to cut and serve. If you haven't one or can't find one to buy, use a 20cm (8 inch) round flan tin instead.

Serve this tasty flan with cherry tomato and bean salad (page 68) and a crisp leafy salad, plus plenty of warm French bread.

410g (13oz) packet shortcrust pastry	*2 eggs*
2 large red peppers, about 375g (12oz) total weight	*large pinch of powdered saffron*
155g (5oz) full-fat soft cheese with garlic and herbs	*2 tablespoons chopped parsley*
	1 tablespoon chopped basil
	salt and pepper to taste
	herb sprigs to garnish

1 Preheat oven to 200C (400F/Gas 6). Roll out the pastry on a lightly floured surface and use to line a 30 × 11cm (12 × 4½ inch) tranche tin. Chill for 15 minutes. Line with greaseproof paper and baking beans and bake blind for about 15 minutes or until the pastry edges are pale golden. Remove the paper and beans and bake for a further 5 minutes to cook the base. Lower oven temperature to 180C (350F/Gas 4).

2 Preheat grill to high and grill the peppers for 10-12 minutes, turning frequently, until the skin is charred. Cool slightly, then rub off the skins under cold running water. Pat dry with absorbent kitchen paper. Halve the peppers, remove core and seeds, then roughly chop the flesh.

3 In a bowl, whisk together the soft cheese, eggs, saffron and herbs until smooth. Stir in the peppers and seasoning. Spoon into the prepared flan case and bake for 25 minutes or until just set. Serve garnished with herbs. *Serves 6.*

NOTE: If you prefer to make your own pastry, use a 185g (6oz/1¼ cup) flour quantity.

Summer Vegetable Salad

60g (2oz) dried pasta shells
250g (8oz) cauliflower florets
125g (4oz) young, small carrots
2 courgettes (zucchini), thickly
   sliced
8 button onions, halved
125g (4oz) French beans
2 tomatoes, peeled, quartered
   and seeded

60g (2 oz / ⅓ cup) black olives
BASIL DRESSING:
90ml (3 fl oz / ⅓ cup) olive oil
2 tablespoons white wine vinegar
1 tablespoon shredded basil
1 clove garlic, crushed
salt and pepper to taste

1 Cook the pasta and all the vegetables (except the tomatoes) separately, in boiling salted water until just tender. Drain and refresh under cold water.
2 In a small pan, whisk together the dressing ingredients and heat gently for 2-3 minutes.
3 Toss together the cooked vegetables, pasta, tomatoes and olives in a serving bowl. Serve immediately. *Serves 6.*

Apple, Leaf & Walnut Salad

6 celery sticks
3 crisp green eating apples
juice of ½ lemon
1 small head frisée (curly
   endive)
1 small bunch lambs' lettuce
   (corn salad)
60g (2oz / ⅔ cup) walnut halves,
   toasted

DRESSING:
60ml (2 fl oz / ¼ cup) walnut oil
60ml (2 fl oz / ¼ cup) olive oil
2 tablespoons white wine vinegar
1 teaspoon wholegrain mustard
salt and pepper to taste

1 Cut the celery into matchstick pieces. Cut the apple into similar-sized pieces and toss in lemon juice.
2 Whisk together the ingredients for the dressing. Just before serving, toss all the salad ingredients and dressing together in a large bowl. *Serves 6.*

Pear & Parmesan Salad

4 ripe figs
3 ripe pears
1 large frisée (curly endive)
30g (1oz / ⅓ cup) walnuts,
    toasted
185g (6oz) Parmesan cheese

DRESSING:
1 tablespoon sherry vinegar
½ teaspoon wholegrain mustard
salt and pepper to taste
60ml (2 fl oz / ¼ cup) olive oil

1 In a bowl, whisk together the ingredients for the dressing.
2 Cut the figs into wedges. Halve, core and slice the pears. Add the fruit to the dressing and stir well to coat.
3 Tear the frisée (endive) into a large salad bowl and add the fruit, dressing and walnuts. Toss lightly to mix.
4 Using a vegetable peeler, pare the Parmesan into thin shavings. Sprinkle over the salad and serve immediately. *Serves 8.*

Spiced Fennel & Avocado Salad

The raw egg yolk in this dressing adds a delicious creaminess but substitute 1 tablespoon of fromage frais if you prefer.

1 bunch spring onions (green
    shallots)
375g (12oz) cherry tomatoes,
    halved
185g (6oz) Florence fennel
2 avocados

DRESSING:
1 egg yolk
½ teaspoon Tabasco sauce
½ teaspoon paprika
salt and pepper to taste
90ml (3 fl oz / ⅓ cup) olive oil
1 tablespoon wholegrain
    mustard

1 In a large bowl, whisk together the dressing ingredients.
2 Cut the spring onions (green shallots) into 2.5cm (1 inch) pieces. Add to the dressing with the tomatoes and stir to mix.
3 Just before serving, thinly slice the fennel. Peel, halve and stone the avocados, then cut into slices. Add the fennel and avocado to the salad and toss well. *Serves 6.*

Bean & Gruyère Salad

500g (1 lb) French beans, halved
250g (8oz) thin leeks, sliced
  lengthwise
500g (1 lb) frozen broad beans
90g (3oz) gruyère cheese, grated

DRESSING:
3 tablespoons white wine
2 tablespoons thin honey
1 teaspoon Dijon mustard
2 tablespoons olive oil
salt and pepper to taste

1 Cook the French beans in a large pan of boiling salted water for about 6 minutes until almost tender. Add the leeks and broad beans and simmer for a further 2 minutes. Drain and transfer to a salad bowl, removing the broad bean skins if time.
2 Whisk together the ingredients for the dressing. Add to the warm vegetables and toss well. Cool, cover and refrigerate for at least 2 hours or overnight.
3 Sprinkle with gruyère to serve. *Serves 6.*

Cherry Tomato & Bean Salad

185g (6oz) broad beans
185g (6oz) French beans, halved
125g (4oz) mozzarella cheese,
  cubed
500g (1 lb) cherry tomatoes,
  halved
tiny basil leaves and/or thyme
  sprigs to taste

DRESSING:
½ red pepper
155ml (5 fl oz / ⅔ cup) olive oil
1 clove garlic, crushed
2 tablespoons dry white wine
2 tablespoons lemon juice
salt and pepper to taste

1 Cook the broad beans in plenty of boiling salted water for about 3 minutes; drain. Cook French beans in boiling salted water for 7-10 minutes; drain.
2 Place the ingredients for the dressing in a food processor or blender and work until smooth. Pour into a salad bowl.
3 Toss in the beans, mozzarella, tomatoes and herbs. Cover and leave for at least 2 hours before serving. *Serves 6.*

Spinach, Corn & Alfalfa Salad

125g (4oz) smoked streaky
bacon, rinds removed
3 teaspoons sunflower oil
30g (1oz / ⅓ cup) pine nuts,
toasted
2 tablespoons red wine

2 tablespoons walnut oil
2 teaspoons red wine vinegar
salt and pepper to taste
125g (4oz) baby corn cobs
250g (8oz) fresh spinach
60g (2oz) alfalfa sprouts

1 Roughly chop bacon. Heat the sunflower oil in a pan and sauté the bacon until crisp and golden. Off the heat, stir in the pine nuts, wine, walnut oil and vinegar. Cool and season.

2 Cook baby corn in boiling salted water for 4-5 minutes until just tender. Drain, cool and halve lengthwise.

3 Tear the spinach leaves into bite-sized pieces and place in a large salad bowl with the alfalfa sprouts and corn. Add the dressing, toss well and serve immediately. *Serves 6.*

Minted Potatoes with Orange

3 oranges
90ml (3 fl oz / ⅓ cup) olive oil
4 teaspoons caster sugar
1 clove garlic, crushed

salt and pepper to taste
1.25kg (2½ lb) small new
potatoes
mint leaves to taste

1 Grate the rind and squeeze the juice of 1 orange. In a medium bowl, whisk together the olive oil, orange rind and juice, sugar, garlic and seasoning.

2 Cook the potatoes in boiling salted water until just tender. Drain well, halve and toss immediately into the dressing. Cover and leave to cool.

3 With a small sharp knife, peel away all rind and pith from the remaining 2 oranges. Cut into segments.

4 Just before serving, toss the orange segments and mint leaves into the salad. *Serves 6.*

Alfalfa & Apple Salad

125g (4oz) mange tout (snow
  peas or sugar snap peas)
2 large crisp eating apples
60g (2oz) alfalfa sprouts
1 bunch watercress, roughly
  chopped
30g (1oz) pine nuts, toasted

DRESSING:
125ml (4 fl oz / 1/4 cup) grapeseed
  oil
2 tablespoons white wine vinegar
2 teaspoons caster sugar
2 teaspoons lemon juice
3 teaspoons mild mustard
salt and pepper to taste

1 Cook the mange tout (or snap peas) in boiling salted water for 1 minute. Refresh under cold water and drain.

2 For the dressing, whisk together all the ingredients in a large bowl.

3 Just before serving, halve, core and thinly slice the apples into the dressing. Add all the remaining salad ingredients and toss lightly. *Serves 6.*

Potato & Watercress Salad

1.25kg (2½ lb) old potatoes
1 bunch watercress, roughly
  chopped
½ cucumber, peeled and sliced
1 small onion, finely chopped

DRESSING:
315ml (10 fl oz / 1¼ cups)
  mayonnaise
125ml (4 fl oz / ½ cup) thick sour
  cream
2 tablespoons creamed
  horseradish
salt and pepper to taste

1 For the dressing, whisk together all the ingredients in a large bowl.

2 Cook the potatoes in boiling salted water until just tender. Drain well, thickly slice and toss immediately into the dressing; allow to cool.

3 Add the watercress, cucumber and onion. Toss lightly to serve. *Serves 8.*

Coconut Rice with Pineapple

This is an excellent combination to use as a 'bed' for a dressed salad such as spiced saffron chicken (page 16). If serving as an accompaniment to cold or simply grilled meats I moisten it with a little French dressing too.

2 tablespoons sunflower oil
1 small onion, finely chopped
1 bay leaf
1 cinnamon stick
2 whole green cardamoms, split
90g (3oz / ½ cup) wild rice
30g (1oz) creamed coconut, grated
salt and pepper to taste
185g (6oz / 1¼ cups) long-grain white rice

2 tablespoons chopped parsley or coriander
30g (1oz / ¼ cup) slivered almonds, toasted
250g (8oz) chopped fresh pineapple
TO GARNISH:
toasted slivers of fresh coconut
coriander sprigs

1 Heat the oil in a large saucepan, add the onion, bay leaf, cinnamon and cardamoms and sauté until the onion is golden.

2 Stir in the wild rice and creamed coconut. Add 1 litre (1¾ pints/4 cups) water and ¼ teaspoon salt. Bring to the boil and simmer for about 20 minutes.

3 Add the long-grain rice and cook for 15 minutes or until the rice is just cooked. Drain, rinse under cold water and drain well.

4 Turn the rice into a large salad bowl and stir in the parsley or coriander, almonds and pineapple. Serve within 2 hours, garnished with toasted coconut and coriander sprigs.

Serves 8.

Sweet Spiced Onions

500g (1 lb) pickling onions or
shallots, peeled and trimmed
155ml (10 fl oz / ⅔ cup)
sunflower oil
2 teaspoons clear honey
1 tablespoon cider vinegar

2 spring onions (green shallots),
finely chopped
2 teaspoons chopped coriander
1 small red chilli, finely sliced
salt and pepper to taste

1 Place the onions in a saucepan and cover with cold water. Bring to the boil, cover and simmer for 15-20 minutes until just tender. Drain and place in a bowl.
2 Meanwhile whisk together the oil, honey and vinegar. Stir into the hot onions with the spring onions (shallots), coriander and chilli. Leave to cool, stirring occasionally. Season before serving. *Serves 6.*

Mixed Grain & Mushroom Salad

Try to use a mix of cultivated and wild mushrooms in this salad. Chanterelles, especially, add a wonderful 'woody' flavour.

125g (4oz) green lentils, soaked
overnight
60g (2oz / ⅓ cup) wild rice
185g (6oz / 1¼ cups) long-grain
white rice
2 tablespoons grapeseed oil
90g (3oz) mushrooms, sliced

2 tablespoons chopped thyme
grated rind and juice of 1 orange
2 tablespoons hazelnut oil
2 tablespoons white wine vinegar
1 tablespoon Dijon mustard
salt and pepper to taste

1 Place the drained lentils and wild rice in a pan of boiling salted water. Boil for 25 minutes before adding the white rice. Cook for a further 15 minutes or until the rice and lentils are just tender. Drain, refresh under cold water and cool.
2 Heat the grapeseed oil in a small pan, add the mushrooms and thyme and sauté for 3-4 minutes. Off the heat, stir in the remaining ingredients. Cool before serving. *Serves 8.*

Mixed Rice & Lentil Pilaff

This is an excellent hot accompaniment for all spicy dishes such as coconut cream chicken (page 42). Don't be tempted to look at the rice before the end of the cooking time or you'll lose valuable steam.

315g (10oz / 2 cups) basmati rice　　*2 whole cloves*
60g (2oz / 1/3 cup) red lentils　　　*2 cinnamon sticks*
30g (1oz) butter　　　　　　　　*1 teaspoon cumin seeds*
185g (6oz) onion, chopped　　　　*2 bay leaves*
2 green cardamoms　　　　　　　*1 teaspoon salt*

1 Put the rice and lentils in a bowl, cover with cold water and leave to soak for 30 minutes.
2 Melt the butter in a large saucepan, add the onion and sauté for 2-3 minutes until golden. Add the spices and bay leaves and sauté for a further 1 minute.
3 Stir in 750ml (24 fl oz / 3 cups) water and the salt. Bring to the boil and add the drained rice and lentils.
4 Cover tightly, lower the heat and simmer gently for 7 minutes. Reduce the heat further and continue to cook very gently for 10-15 minutes or until the water has been absorbed and the rice is tender. Fork through before serving. *Serves 8*.

Index